# Top Hunters

Written by Claire Llewellyn

## Collins

## What is a hunter?

Hunters are animals that catch other animals for food. Hunters may be little or large but they are all specially adapted to kill. They have powerful muscles and excellent senses to help them.

excellent **vision**

powerful muscles

sharp **talons**

sleek shape

serrated teeth

excellent sense of smell

## Gaboon vipers

This giant viper wriggles into leaves on the forest floor.
It lies here patiently until a rat or bird comes by.
The snake then plunges its fangs into its **prey**,
injecting a deadly **toxin**.

Gaboon viper

**Did you know?**
The fangs measure the same as a man's thumb.

5

## Lions

Lions usually hunt in a pack. They move silently, with lots of **concentration**. They creep up on animals such as zebras and buffalo. Then suddenly, the lions all race forwards and pounce.

**Did you know?**
Lions are the only big cats that live in groups, called prides.

## Praying mantis

The praying mantis is a successful predator. It hides itself on plants. It keeps so still that insects don't know it's there. In a flash, the mantis snatches them with its spiky front **limbs**.

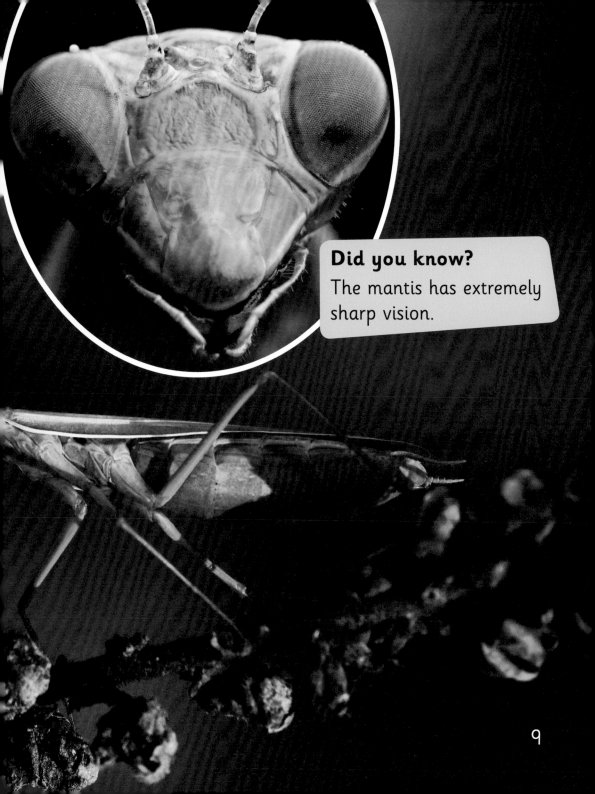

**Did you know?**
The mantis has extremely sharp vision.

## Harpy eagles

Harpy eagles are the largest eagles on Earth. They have a crescent-shaped beak and long talons like knives. When harpy eagles **dive-bomb** small mammals, they have little chance of escape.

10

**Did you know?**
A harpy eagle's foot
measures the same
as a human hand.

## Polar bears

Polar bears can smell seals under the ice. They wait patiently next to a seal's breathing hole.

**Did you know?**
Polar bears have webbed feet.

When a seal comes up for air, the bear knocks it and pulls it out.

breathing hole

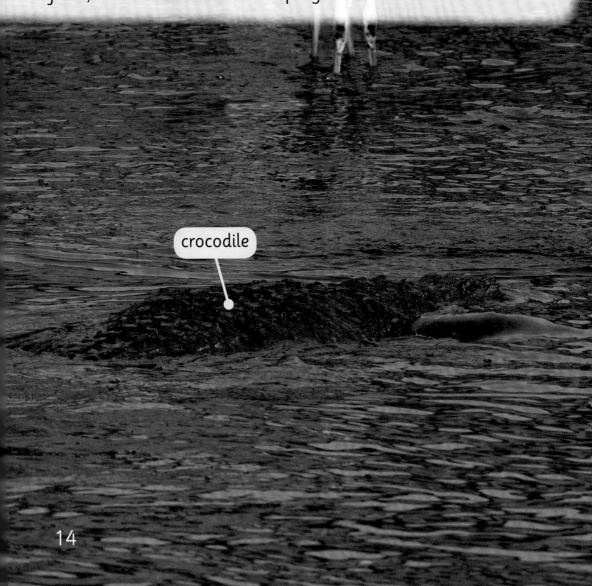

## Crocodiles

Crocodiles have a fearsome reputation. They lie low in rivers, ready to **ambush** animals.

All of a sudden, they lunge forwards, snap their scissor-like jaws, and wrestle with their prey.

crocodile

deer

**Did you know?**
Crocodiles have
the strongest bite
of any animal in
the world.

## Sharks

Usually sharks hunt by following the scent of fish and other sea animals. Sometimes they eat sea birds and seals. When their prey swims into a shark's vision, they hurtle up and attack.

**Did you know?**
There are over 400 different types of sharks!

## The hunting life

Hunters have to catch every meal they eat. Hunting sessions are tiring. A hunter can never be sure of success.

Prey may be rare or it might fight back. Hunters are at risk of kicks and bites. This is why they need the special tools they have to help them catch food.

## Glossary

**ambush** wait to make an attack

**concentration** close attention

**dive-bomb** swoop down from the air

**limbs** arms or legs

**prey**  animals a hunter eats

**talons**  sharp claws

**toxin**  poison

**vision**  sight

# How do these hunters catch food?

Gaboon viper

praying mantis

shark

polar bear

harpy eagle

lion

crocodile

23

# After reading

**Letters and Sounds:** Phases 5–6

**Word count:** 480

**Focus phonemes:** /n/ kn /m/ mb /r/ wr /s/ c, ce, sc /zh/ s, si /sh/ ti, ci, ssi, s

**Common exception words:** of, to, the, into, are, do, their, move, any

**Curriculum links:** Science: Animals, including humans

**National Curriculum learning objectives:** Reading/word reading: apply phonic knowledge and skills as the route to decode words, read accurately by blending sounds in unfamiliar words containing GPCs that have been taught; read other words of more than one syllable that contain taught GPCs; Reading/comprehension: develop pleasure in reading, motivation to read, vocabulary and understanding by discussing word meanings

## Developing fluency

- Your child may enjoy hearing you read the book.
- Take turns to read a page, encouraging your child to read all the "Did you know?" boxes with appropriate intonation for the question and fact.

## Phonic practice

- Challenge your child to read the following, listening for the /sh/ and /zh/ sounds and identifying the letters that make them:

  concentration    vision    measure    patiently    sessions    specially

- Can your child find another word with the /sh/sound but with a different spelling on page 18? (sure)

## Extending vocabulary

- How many words can your child create using the suffixes below (or other suffixes they can think of)?

  strong    hunt    sharp

  -er    -ing    -ly    -est    -ed

- Suggest they check their spellings in a dictionary and then create a sentence using one or two of their new words.